HARMONY

Stewart, Tabori & Chang
NEW YORK

Living together

HOW COUPLES CREATE DESIGN HARMONY AT HOME

ERICA LENNARD AND DENIS COLOMB

WITH TEXT BY JULIA SZABO

contents

ERICA + DENIS = HARMONY

introduction

ERICA LENNARD
DENIS COLOMB

Marriage is a lifelong project. So is creating a home together. Whether you marry early in life and move into your home away from home, or you've been together for many years and shared several homes, many issues arise when two loving individuals decide to live together.

.

Can they successfully integrate the stuff of their previous lives? How can they arrive at important design decisions together? What compromises must be made to achieve domestic bliss? When should one partner yield to another's desires? How to incorporate a piece of furniture that one person cannot stand, but the other cannot live without? How are private spaces agreed upon? How can shared spaces (such as bathrooms) be configured for maximum harmony?

In conceiving and putting together this book, we were naturally inspired by our own experience. When we first met, we were an unlikely match. One of us, namely Erica, had an irrepressible penchant for the neoclassical and baroque. She would scour flea markets and fill her Paris apartment with decorative fabrics and objects from her travels to India, Japan, and Morocco. It was a woman's world full of warmth, vibrant colors, curves, and inviting nooks.

Denis, on the other hand, favored a stringently minimal style, with masculine, ultramodern details such as a curved steel counter and industrial-strength bookcases-on-wheels, plus museum-quality modernist icons such as Warren Platner chairs and Eero Saarinen end tables. The only colors in his place were black, white, and the occasional hint of beige.

Designwise we were an odd couple indeed! And yet, the opposites-attract theory held true. Each of us was immediately drawn to the other's home—probably because our places were so clearly a pure reflection of ourselves.

The power of that attraction is what enabled us to marry our disparate styles in every place we've lived, creating a successful synthesis of each other's tastes. The result is a mixture of antique and modern, cool metal and warm wood, neutral tones and vibrant color. With a little editing and a lot of patience, our most treasured belongings now share pride of place in our current home in Los Angeles. And it's a place we truly love coming home to.

Since we first came together our tastes have evolved a great deal. Denis, for instance, has embraced warmth and color, which can be seen in a whole new line of home furnishing products that he has created. He developed various pieces, including a Moghul-inspired wooden day bed, specifcally for our current home. The house reminds us of our shared love for India: its architecture, climate, light, and outdoor spaces. (And, after years of photographing other people's gardens all over the world, Erica finally has one of her own.)

We have had the good fortune to meet couples all over the world that successfully share their own personal environments. The 15 couples featured in this book have inspired us in our life and our work, and we have learned so much from them. Of course, many of them are design professionals, so they have an advantage when it comes to creating gorgeous homes. But everywhere we look in magazines, in films, and even on the television we see people finding new ways to create harmony in their environment. What is more, we see a real interest on the part of life partners to participate in all aspects of design, from deciding where to live, to designating what rooms will be used for what purpose, to even more mundane tasks such as choosing doorknobs.

Not too long ago making a house a home was by definition a woman's job (unless, of course, the man was a professional decorator) and the more stereotypically macho task of home improvement was a man's domain. Those days, however, are over. Men and women are equally active on the home-design front with men displaying a strong interest in choosing furniture styles—a short time ago they only felt comfortable choosing stereo and other electronic equipment. Today it's not uncommon to see young couples cheerfully browsing for decorative home furnishings together.

Even something as historically controversial as the color pink now has genuine appeal for both sexes thanks to what we have discovered from the ancient art of feng shui. Feng shui master R. D. Chin frequently counsels couples to paint a "relationship" wall in their home a vibrant rose, to keep them "in the pink." We have been enormously inspired by our travels across India, where we gained an appreciation of Vaastu, the ancient Hindu science of architectural alignment by which buildings and interiors are laid out to complement the earth's energies.

But all this is just a contemporary spin on an old story. History tells us of many very different couples whose lifestyles have merged in romantic, poetic surroundings: Vanessa Bell and Duncan Grant, Sonia and Robert Delaunay, Russel and Mary Wright, Charles and Ray Eames—these and many more created homes that were true reflections of their identity as couples.

Sometimes when two extraordinary people come together, the result can have serious historic repercussions. Half a century ago, the Eameses and Wrights used their respective homes as a laboratory for ideas that would influence the way many of us decorate today. In a spare bedroom in their California home, the Eameses experimented with the wood molding that would become their design legacy as well as a fixture in many of today's most glamorous interiors. "Good informal living substitutes a little headwork for a lot of legwork," Russel Wright once said. "It doesn't need wealth, but it does take thought, some ingenuity and resourcefulness, and more than a little loving care to create a home that is really your own." The loving care the Eameses and Wrights lavished on their own homes has been especially inspiring to us, as have the beautifully appointed residences of Christian and Elizabeth de Portzamparc, Charles and Marie-Laure de Noailles, Ismail Merchant and James Ivory, and Lella and Massimo Vignelli.

But a couple's home needn't be extravagant to inspire; it needn't even be a permanent home. John Lennon and Yoko Ono moved us with their ability to set up house

wherever they went. Such was the force of their togetherness that it made even a hotel bed home. We put the couples profiled here in the same league. They've successfully joined their individual lives, which itself is no small feat. On top of that, they have managed to merge their lifestyles, expressing their love through passionate interior design and creating homes as harmonious as they are visually stunning.

We hope the aesthetic choices they've made together will inspire you to create a home that expresses your true identity as a couple. Remember, it is not just about mixing and matching styles or tastes. It is a fundamental joining of two souls under one roof—and that is what enables perfect harmony.

PRECEDING PAGES (4)
Scenes from a marriage of styles: the left column shows three rooms of Erica's neo-baroque 19th-century Paris apartment, before we met. The center column shows three views of Denis's minimalist Parisian loft. At right, and on page 7, in our first shared place on the rue de Rivoli, we merged our individual aesthetics to create a new look that manages to reflect both our decorative passions.

(7) Erica's warm woods and colorful textiles merge with Denis's cool metals and neutral tones to create a harmonious environment.
OPPOSITE Our new Los Angeles residence in the Hollywood Hills—a Spanish colonial-style house. Here we have taken the blending of our very different styles a step further. This is an ideal setting for those whose tastes are as distinctively different as ours were.

style soulmates

allegra & ashley hicks

Some couples must work at achieving a harmonious blend of disparate styles. Then there are those blessed with nearly identical aesthetic values. For these partners, collaborating on decor is a seemingly effortless exercise. The result of such a marriage of styles? Beautiful interiors that are much more than photogenic rooms; they are genuine love nests, where romance flourishes and matrimony thrives.

The enormously creative Ashley and Allegra Hicks are an enviable example. Designwise, they are perfectly matched: Ashley designs interiors and a collection of furniture called Jantar Mantar, while his wife, the Italian-born Allegra, creates interiors, textiles, and fashion (she also owns an eponymous lifestyle store on London's Chelsea Green as well as a design showroom in Chelsea Harbour Design Center selling everything from home furnishings to clothing).

Both separately and as a unit, this glamorous pair has graced the pages of the world's most elegant fashion and shelter magazines. One might expect such a dynamic design duo to be mindful of their high profiles, creating a home that doubles as a

showhouse. That's definitely not the case with this couple. Their place is a wonderfully warm townhouse in London's Chelsea.

"It's very important to have personal things in your decor," Ashley explains. "At the end of the day, if a home isn't personal, what's it for? One is so used to seeing decorated houses that have been purged of all personality until they end up looking like a resort hotel!"

Here's one charming way he personalized the space he shares with his wife: "I make little Ganesha shrines and put them all around the house," Ashley says, referring the Hindu elephant god of wisdom and good fortune. "Unknowingly, Allegra and I were married on Ganesha's festival day, the eighteenth of October. When we went to India on our honeymoon, we were told that the date was very auspicious, and that we'd be very lucky. So that's why we have Ganeshas everywhere."

The Hickses are an inspiration to design professionals and the decoratively challenged alike. Their home is just as dashing as they are. In every room, on every floor, there is ample evidence of the magical union of two creatively compatible temperaments.

The living room is a fine example of what happens when the styles of two individuals marry happily to become one. An ottoman Allegra designed to look like an upside-down jester's cap is covered in a gorgeous red embroidered fabric that the couple discovered in Fez, Morocco. Nearby are two unique coffee tables, one designed by Ashley and the other by Allegra, that appear to engage in an agreeable, if not downright romantic conversation despite their very different looks (his has a metal base and round wood top, while hers features a parchment square atop a copper base made to resemble a fleur-de-lis). Anchoring it all underfoot is one of the striking dhurrie rugs Allegra is known for, its abstract pattern composed of free-form circles.

A cozy townhouse
in London's Chelsea

PRECEDING PAGES (10)
In the living room, the Drum
table is from Ashley's Jantar
Mantar collection; The Spheres
rug is Allegra's design.

(12-13) The living room: a
happy marriage of style.
ABOVE Wallpaper festooned
with double A's covers the stairway walls; the banisters and rail-
ings were created by the couple's
designer friend Tom Dixon.
OPPOSITE The living room
with a portrait of King Edward
VII reflected in the mirror.

In the bedroom one finds a closet with mirrored doors that's a dream come true for a passionate clothes horse. Rather than complain about her acquisitions, Allegra's husband paid romantic tribute by building her a place to keep them in. "It's all mine," she says of the closet. "He likes to throw away clothes; I don't. Like every woman in the world who piles up clothes from the age of twenty-two, I didn't have any room left. I'm always thinking, Oh, this Romeo Gigli coat will be great for my kids in fifteen years! Plus, I have a collection of my mother's old shoes, they're beautiful. So I needed some extra storage space, and Ashley built this closet for me. It even has two drawers under-neath just for shoes. The mirrors make it work very well in the room, without overwhelming it."

On the rare occasions that Ashley and Allegra have dis-agreed, the solution ends up being an extraordinary contribu-tion to the home. Case in point: what to put on the walls by the stairs. When they first moved into the house ten years ago, Allegra originally envisioned those hallways painted white, but Ashley disagreed, knowing the high-traffic area would quickly get soiled. "I was quite impractical about it," Allegra admits now, "because I'd mostly lived in flats. But Ashley was adamant about having wallpaper. He explained that in a house, you spend so much time going up and down, you basically live on the stairs, and the walls get ruined. Wallpaper disguises it quite beautifully. He was right: Nine years later, the wallpaper is still beautiful, but if we'd had white walls, we'd have had to paint it at least ten times."

Of course, this being one of the world's most creative cou-ples, theirs isn't any ordinary wallpaper pattern. To honor his wife's love of alchemy symbols, Ashley designed a sage-green fantasia of mazes and doves flying into bottles. He added an extra romantic flourish: repeating, entwined double A's (their

shared first initial). More than just a practical solution to a problem that plagues all multilevel house dwellers, it's a charming valentine that the couple has enjoyed every day for the past ten years. "It has a very calming effect," Allegra says. "It's like you can solve your life by looking at this wallpaper." In the library is another everyday valentine: the hand-painted frieze that crowns the shelves. "It depicts a romantic message from me to her in coded Italian," Ashley explains. "I drew the letters out, but she had to paint it herself," he recalls with a laugh. "Somehow, that takes the romance out of it." Actually, he's wrong. It's just one more wonderfully offbeat and deeply romantic collaborative effort from a couple that's perfected the art of living together.

RIGHT The kitchen (top); the library frieze, with its secret message from Ashley to Allegra (bottom).
OPPOSITE The dining room is made charming by Allegra's *trompe l'oeil* fresco depicting a picture window with floating curtain.

FOLLOWING PAGES (18-19) Clockwise from left: The bedroom, with its romantic corona in the style of David Hicks, Ashley's decorator father, with coral jewelry designed by Ashley for Allegra in the foreground; the library and the bedroom with pillows designed by Allegra.

common grounds

harmonious how-to's

• Don't expect a harmonious living arrangement to materialize overnight. As with anything else in a relationship, it takes time. Believe it or not, the Hickses' place wasn't always picture perfect. They moved to their home with "an existing sofa" rather than buying a new one before they figured out what their needs were. According to Ashley, "It's good not to make too many commitments at an early stage. Move in without doing too much and slowly see what you can find in the house—and in each other."

• Keep romance alive by making your sleeping quarters as wonderfully intimate as possible, especially if you have a mattress that's king-size or larger. Curtains or a corona—a signature item popularized by the great decorator David Hicks, Ashley's late father—turn the bed into a love-tent that's yours alone. Even the sheerest mosquito netting can bring a wonderful sense of privacy to your bedroom, shielding it from the rest of the home and the world like the sacred space it is. The Hickses' bed is tented by four swags of fabric suspended by a ceiling-mounted corona.

• Commemorations of your love are meaningful, wonderful accessories in an interior, whether they're framed wedding photographs or flea-market finds you unearthed together. However, limit couple and family photographs to the bedroom. "Family and wedding photographs should be kept out of the reception rooms," Ashley advises. "I find they can slightly take over, and it's a little difficult for guests to stare at all these pictures of you at various stages of your life." In their bedroom, a subtle personal touch comes from the beautiful coral pieces created by Ashley that were his gifts to Allegra. On the bed is a charming little pillow with a hand-painted "AA."

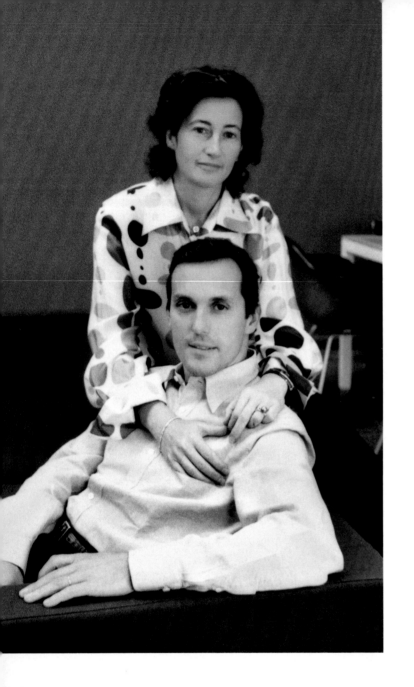

Busy Paris-based architect-designer Florence Baudoux has such a hectic schedule that when her business executive husband, Aldo Fabiani, spotted an ad in *Le Figaro* for a loft, she had no time to go and investigate his find. So Aldo went alone to scout the place, a former ballet studio, and came home with an intriguing appraisal: "It is a very nice place, but it needs a lot of work." Sensing a challenge, Florence made time to have a look, and when she saw the long, narrow space with its high, high ceilings and towering windows, "I said to myself, I know exactly what we are going to do here." What they did was transform it into one of Paris' most striking contemporary residences.

Deferring to his wife's design talent and experience, Aldo was happy to give Florence free reign to treat their new home as her canvas. But it was more than a creative outlet: It was the start of a new business. Inspired by the loft's unusual dimensions—and frustrated that she could find few furnishings big and bold enough to work in such a massive space—Florence designed many of the oversize items that now comprise her brilliant furniture collection, oom.

classic meets modern

florence baudoux &
aldo fabiani

Among her ingenious creations: a long, narrow coffee table with a colorfully lacquered tray top, an extra-long striped sofa with steel legs, and ceiling-light fixtures that look like illuminated UFOs yet perfectly complement the space's original moldings. "You need flying saucers in a space like this!" she explains. Her creations blend beautifully with the couple's other iconic furnishings, including chairs by the Eames and Paul Kjerholm and a Cappellini sofa. Florence's taste is quite specific: She is a strict minimalist, and never displays flowers, plants, artwork, or family photos at home. The only nonessential items in the place are the couple's collection of 1960s ceramic vases. She says she was inspired to live this way by the time she spent in the loft before she undertook the renovations. "When we moved in, we had sold all our furniture except for a table, chairs, and a bed," she says. "The first night I slept there, I said, 'This is fantastic, to live without anything! We're going to live like this!'" Although wary at first about living so minimally, the ever-agreeable Aldo

now feels "very happy" there. "It's great to have all this space," he says. "You feel really free, because you don't have a lot of things that you don't need."

One thing Aldo couldn't live without was a first-rate stereo system. "He loves listening to music," says his wife. "It's the first thing he does when he comes home from work, because it's his favorite way to relax." The audio equipment (by BW and Meridian) was Aldo's choice, but the gigantic speakers are an eyesore to Florence. "I wanted Bang and Olufsen ones because they are so pretty," she admits. "They are pretty," Aldo agrees, "but they're not the highest fidelity." She's glad he put his foot down: "When you hear the sound coming from those speakers, you've really heard everything—it's incredible," says Florence.

So what if the big, black monoliths are not the most attractive feature in the room? Next on Florence's to-do list is designing a clever way to conceal them. And knowing her, that might just lead to a brilliant new business, too.

A minimalist apartment in Paris

PRECEDING PAGE (21)
The living room, with sofa and coffee tables designed by Florence that were the inspiration for oom, her home furnishings collection.
OPPOSITE Aldo's stereo equipment dominates the living room.
FOLLOWING PAGES (24)
This stainless-steel stairway leads to the bedroom.
(25) The elaborate moldings are all that remains of the former dance studio, which Florence has modernized completely.
(26) The bathroom includes his-and-hers closets; his is extremely organized (top). The Italian glass-topped dinning table on a steel frame was custom-made for Florence (bottom).
(27) The 1960s vases by Ruellan always stand empty. A strict minimalist, Florence does not like flowers. "My husband knows me well enough not to bring me flowers," she says.

common grounds

harmonious how-to's

• Work together to agree on paint colors that appeal to both of you. Don't press your luck with controversial colors, especially ones that are too overtly feminine. A fine example of a gender-neutral shade: the handsome, and very practical, deep khaki-green wall Florence and Aldo agreed on.

• If you have different styles of organization, divide up living space where it really counts: the closet. *Chez* Florence and Aldo, there's an uncommon reversal of roles—his closet space is bigger than hers, and every item on his side is meticulously organized, from shirts to shoes, with plenty of space between his tailor-made suits to allow them to breathe. Florence, on the other hand, prefers more avant-garde clothes than her husband, and doesn't mind jamming her Comme des Garçons pieces up against her Isabel Marants.

• If you can't hide your electronic equipment, try to arrange it as appealingly as possible. Florence loves the way her husband's speakers sound but hates the way they look. Until she devises a better solution, they stand like tall sculptures on either side of the wide-screen plasma TV—which, incidentally, looks like a framed, high-tech painting.

the three-month miracle

lisa lovatt-smith & anthony allen

Design authority Lisa Lovatt-Smith has chronicled some of the world's most attractive homes in her numerous books on interior design. She and artist Anthony Allen have made a beautiful home outside Barcelona, transforming a ruin of a house into a place of breathtaking beauty with imagination as the main ingredient.

"The house is very big, with five bedrooms, but it was falling to pieces, so it was incredibly cheap even though it's a listed building of architectural note," Lisa explains. "It had no roof, there were rats and birds everywhere, the plumbing and electricity were from 1927, and it was full of soot from an open fireplace in the kitchen." It takes a visionary to see past serious drawbacks like those. Happily, that's Anthony's forte. "I suggested that we go and look at the house," he says. "And that was the beginning of a big adventure for both of us. It was a lot to take on, but I knew we could fix it up if we were creative as we went along."

With a little help from their friends, the couple completed the renovations in an astonishing three months. "We spent all our money on fixing the house," Lisa says. "After that, we had no money left to decorate!"

Lisa and Anthony are long on ideas and resourcefulness.

A restored landmark house in Barcelona

PRECEDING PAGE (29)
This well-worn treasure of a sofa
embodies the couple's aesthetic.
Above it hangs one of Anthony's
paintings.
OPPOSITE Brioche the dog
lounges on a striped French day
bed (top). The kitchen is a fantasia
of local, colored glazed ceramic
tiles (bottom).
RIGHT A glimpse of the living
room, and another painting by
Anthony, through glass doors
that are original to the house.

Even while we were photographing the dining room, Lisa was suddenly inspired to paint designs in white on the yellow velvet chairs, and so she did! The interior she and Anthony created is an inspired melange of flea-market finds and salvaged items, plus gifts from friends and family.

Anthony's handiwork is evident throughout, from the rotating exhibit of paintings in the lounge where the couple entertains art collectors to the boldly painted walls. Anthony used fine-art pigments for a stunning color-saturated effect. Aware of Lisa's fond nostalgia for Morocco, he chose a palette of vibrant Marrakesh hues. The romance of the gesture was not lost on Lisa: "If you took away all the furniture, you'd still have a great house; the walls just make people gasp."

A project as major as this can quickly put unwanted strain on a partnership. However, Anthony asserts, "We had a great time doing it and it was really good for our relationship. It was a big responsibility to share, and it brought us together because we had to support each other. We were both determined to get it done in a very short period of time, on a budget. It's a big achievement, and we're lucky because we're both still young and fit enough to enjoy it! Your home is more than just a house; it's something that grows with you." Lisa agrees. "If I meet someone and bring them here, it's like I don't have to explain who we are as a couple or what we're about, because it's obvious. The house is the best possible three-dimensional expression of us together: fun, lighthearted, kind of exotic and pretty, but not too serious."

PRECEDING PAGE (32)
The dining room, with a grouping of paintings by Anthony and chairs that the ever-creative Lisa painted right before we shot this picture.
OPPOSITE The deep-blue hallway opens onto the sunny bedroom.
LEFT The "circus-tent" bedroom, with its fuchsia-tented bed (top) and saffron wall hung with Moroccan images by Hervé van der Straten (bottom).
FOLLOWING PAGES (36-37)
Clockwise from top: The bathroom has a antique basin found at a Barcelona flea market and striped wall combined with colored and varnished cement; the hallway is lined with photographs by Jean Loup Sieff, David Bailey, and others; In the living room, a brass Moroccan tea tray and a local decorative ceramic plate alongside a charmingly distressed chair set against a vibrant pink-hued wall.

common grounds

harmonious how-to's

• Lisa and Anthony worked wonders by doing all the work themselves and refusing to spend more than $50 for any one furnishing. So don't look at a tight budget as a constraint; it can actually force you to be more creative and hands-on than you ever thought you were.

• Don't be afraid to move into a tumbledown place; if you fix it up bit by bit, there won't be as much pressure for things to be perfect right away and you won't suffer the angst of being between homes.

• "Paint can really change the proportions and mood of a room," Lisa says. "So be brave with color. I know I could never live in a white house!"

There is something very magical about handmade tiles. Because they are fashioned of clay or similar materials, they recall the most ancient and enduring myths of creation. Wherever handmade tiles are applied in a home, the resulting surface is very appealing, both visually and to the touch, and lends a sense of meaningful permanence. Laying down tiles is more than just a decorating flourish; it's putting down roots.

"It's fantastic to walk barefoot on tiles," says Martine Murat, who lives with her architect husband, Christian Berthéas, in Aix-en-Provence. Together, they produce a collection of unique cement tiles called Carocim (in French, tile is *carreau* and cement is *ciment*—hence the name). The advantage of cement tiles over their ceramic counterparts, Christian explains, is that "they are much less shiny, and they stay warm to the touch, unlike ceramic, which feels cold." Besides looking lustrous and feeling cozy, cement tiles can also be laid closer together than ceramic ones, so they require less grout between tiles and yield an almost painterly effect.

The couple's home serves as a kind of laboratory for their colorful and inventive wares. Immediately upon entering, visitors to Christian and Martine's place are greeted by stunning

matrimonial mosaic
martine murat &
christian berthéas

examples of Carocim artistry. One's eye is immediately drawn to the floors which showcase a wide variety of decorative tiles. But this is no impersonal decorator showhouse; this is a deeply personal space filled with souvenirs of the couple's travels.

The front entrance hallway is paved with pebbles set in concrete that create the effect of very unusual "tiles" that feel like small cobblestones underfoot. After a few steps, one discovers a rectangular mosaic of smooth, flat, blue tiles, bordered with patterned tiles, that cleverly simulates a decorative carpet (one that will never get dirty or slide across the floor!). These dazzling floors are reminiscent of Morocco, a favorite destination for these two frequent flyers. In fact, many of the furnishings in the couple's home were acquired on their many visits to Marrakesh, where beautiful decorative tiles are part of the everyday landscape.

The long corridor leading to the backdoor showcases the couple's impressive collection of masks and boots, as well as a colorful floor that's a Mondrianesque arrangement of tiles in various warm yellows and oranges. This floor recalls the sultry heat of Mexico, another of the couple's favorite destinations,

and the tiles are appropriately jazzy, for Christian is also a jazz musician (his many drums and guitars are strewn all over the house). In the bedroom, the house's existing terra-cotta floors were enlivened by the addition of Carocim tiles in sky blue, pink, yellow, violet, and green.

Most of us live with tiles in the kitchen or bathroom, and even then most common tiles tend to be quite plain. But because extraordinary tiles appear everywhere *chez* Christian and Martine, it is not surprising to find that the kitchen floor is paved with especially extraordinary tiles whose scrollwork design is based on a 1924 Art Deco pattern.

Floors are not the only tiled surfaces here. In the living room, the large coffee table was hand-tiled by Martine in a black-and-white checkerboard pattern, complete with a two-dimensional centerpiece of orange and red flowers on top. And in the laundry room, sinuous bird-shaped tiles fly along the cement walls, while squares adorned with ceramic frogs, turtles, and crabs crawl underfoot.

These playful Carocims were inspired by the couple's love of all animals; they currently have four cats, one dog, and at least 28 birds, including parrots and finches. Actually, the only room in the place that isn't tiled is the aviary that houses the birds' cages. But that will soon change, Martine promises. "There just isn't enough time!"

A house of tiles in Provence

LEFT The couple surrounds themselves with tile artistry as in the bedroom sitting area. The original terra-cotta tiles have been enlivened with Carocim tiles (top). In the living room (bottom), the large coffee table has a black-and-white checkerboard pattern with a two-dimensional floral centerpiece.

OPPOSITE A Moroccan door and animal-theme tiles enliven the laundry room. Whimsical bird-shaped tiles fly along the cement wall, while squares adorned with ceramic creatures crawl underfoot.

common grounds

harmonious how-to's

• Handmade tiles are becoming more and more popular all over the world, and with good reason. As more and more of us decorate with tiles, it's time to realize that they're not just for the kitchen and bathroom any more; they bring an air of timeless beauty to any room in the home, and they're enormously practical. After all, what could be better than a tiled cocktail table that virtually eliminates the need for coasters!

• Handmade tiles are something many couples can agree on, for they are neither too feminine nor too masculine. Plus, tiles have great allure for people with vastly different tastes, who otherwise might have trouble agreeing on decorative materials.

• Couples with children and/or pets or those planning families particularly appreciate tiled surfaces in the home because they are easy to keep clean. And as many have learned the hard way, simple, low-maintenance surfaces can help to cut down on domestic disputes.

LEFT Wall-to-wall art deco-patterned tiles: On the kitchen floor (top) and all over the kitchen (bottom).
OPPOSITE Christian, a musician, moved into Martine's home bringing only his instruments.

patricia tartour &
philippe jonathan

fellow travelers

Not many people would buy an abandoned quarry, parts of which date back to ancient Roman times, and transform it, indoors and out, to create a family compound. But Philippe Jonathan and Patricia Tartour are no ordinary couple. Their extraordinary passion for what they do—he is an architect, she is a travel consultant-informs everything in their lives, and extends to their wonderfully unique place in Provence. "Doing a house together is like having a child," agree both halves of this couple, who have raised three daughters together. "This house is our fourth child."

With an apartment in Paris as a home base, Philippe and Patricia had no intention of purchasing a house. But after renting summer homes in the Luberon region for several years, they thought they might as well start looking to buy. After several attempts, they couldn't find anything that moved them. Then one day, Patricia recalls, "The realtor said, 'I think I have something for you: it's a crazy place for crazy people!' What he showed them was a limestone quarry with four small stone bungalows. Looking out over the whole Luberon park from the vantage point of a small stone bench perched on a hill, they knew

At home in a Provençal stone quarry

PRECEDING PAGE (47)
The living room, with furnishings brought back from Thailand, China, India, and Burma.
LEFT Philippe's office, carved out of limestone (top). Simple stone structures dot the property—this one houses the bedroom and private living room (bottom).
OPPOSITE The remains of the stone quarry remind Philippe and Patricia of the great temples of Angkor Wat. The sofa Patricia loves (which Philippe doesn't care for) is relegated to the periphery.

it was for them. "We looked at each other," Patricia says, "and we knew we would be very happy here."

A very important part of the property's appeal was its openness to the elements. The landscape and clouds reminded Philippe and Patricia of China. It was their appreciation of China that brought them together; both had spent a lot of time traveling there, and both speak fluent Chinese. It would turn out to be the ultimate work-in-progress—a project that, like marriage, never ends. "As a couple, you have to build permanently together," Patricia says. "This is the meaning of living together. When you stop having children, buying a house or doing an interesting project like this is a kind of guarantee that you will always share a common goal."

The tumbledown grandeur of the place, its vast size and almost monastic emptiness, has inspired certain follies. When they travel, Philippe and Patricia tend to shop in expansive proportions; one of Patricia's business ventures is an Asian home-furnishings boutique in Paris called L'Esprit Chine. Even before they bought this property, they were prone to bringing back shipping containers of furniture from their frequent trips to Asia. But now, because of their home's almost limitless dimensions, they can pretty much let their imaginations run wild. From terra-cotta jars to teak furnishings, metalwork to mirrors, the exceptional objects gathered here come from China, Burma, Cambodia, Sri Lanka, and Rajasthan.

However, Philippe and Patricia travel a lot less than they used to: The home they've made for themselves keeps them happily anchored. As Philippe concludes, "This kind of place makes you see things with a big perspective."

PRECEDING PAGES (50) Chinese tea in the afternoon shade on a walkway between two of the many houses that make up the compound.

(51) The wilderness of the terrain is what first attracted the couple to their home; they have deliberately left it undisturbed.

OPPOSITE The guest bedroom, with its original stone wall left intact.

FOLLOWING PAGES (54) The minimal interiors are at once ancient and modern.

(55) When the couple first met, each had one wooden Chinese chest that had great personal meaning, revealing their shared passion for Asia; this one is Patricia's (top). The bedroom, with its rounded windows inspired by the architecture of Tunisia, where Patricia grew up (bottom).

common grounds

harmonious how-to's

• Listen to each other's ideas and respect each other's needs and tastes. Philippe is an architect, yet he didn't impose his own plans across the board. Many details in the couple's home were designed as tributes to Patricia. For instance, the rounded windows in the bedroom were inspired by the architecture of Tunisia, where she grew up.

• Having this much space cannot help but lend itself to harmonious living. On the rare occasion that they disagree about an item of furniture, Philippe and Patricia don't have to resort to giving it away, or selling it, or putting it in storage. As is the case with a pair of baroque Dutch Colonial-style sofas that Philippe cannot stand but Patricia could not live without, they now live at the entrance to the quarry building, where she can enjoy them and he doesn't have to be bothered by them.

• Sometimes, a work-in-progress doesn't have to be completely finished to be spectacular. To some eyes, the Tartour-Jonathan compound looks like an archaeological ruin, but they look at it and see their beloved home.

Irene and Giorgio Silvagni have inspired us for more than 20 years. He is a film producer; she is a woman of great style who works as the creative director for the avant-garde Japanese designer Yohji Yamamoto. Together, they restored a 17th-century house in the South of France to become one of the world's most admired and photographed interiors–the archetype of what everyone wants in a Provençal home. Their friends from all over the world look forward to visiting them there, for the Silvagnis are also wonderful hosts. Besides being beautiful, their place is so intensely personal, so clearly a reflection of Irene and Giorgio, that even if you find yourself alone there, you can feel their presence. This house has *soul*.

There is nothing more magical than falling in love with a house together: It's like falling in love all over again. That's precisely what happened to Irene and Giorgio. When they first saw their "sleeping beauty" of a house, it took their breath away, even though it had been abandoned, the windows were boarded

a new beginning

irene & giorgio silvagni

up, and their first glimpse of the interior was by flashlight. Reawakening the sleeping beauty was a true labor of love, and a joint effort. Irene adores flea-marketing, and is usually up at the crack of dawn scouring *les puces* every weekend. Years of practice have perfected her game, and she's filled the place with extraordinary treasures, to the playful consternation of her husband.

"I am sort of an alcoholic of buying," she explains with a laugh, indicating a screen separating the couple's bedroom from their bathroom, which practically groans under the weight of Irene's vintage textile collection, which is impressive and growing all the time. "I love old lace, costumes, and textiles from Japan, China, India, Russia . . . and I like to leave my things out, so I can look at them. At least once a week my husband says to me, 'When are you taking all that crap away?' or 'When are you opening a shop?' It's a game between us, and it's been going on like that for thirty years!"

Where Irene's passion is hunting and gathering, Giorgio's is hands-on decorating. When the couple first moved their furniture into the house, everything they brought with them was

A maison de famille in the South of France

PRECEDING PAGE (57)
The upstairs landing, between the guest room and master bedroom.
OPPOSITE The view from the master bedroom.
RIGHT Personal spaces for private times: his swimming pool (top), her beloved garden (bottom) adorned with a chandelier designed by Giorgio.

stolen one day while they were out, including a Louis XIII chest with original gilding that was especially dear to Giorgio. After that, Giorgio says, he and Irene agreed "never again to buy things of value. Instead, we started to buy very common things that we painted and modified, and they have a lot of allure." Giorgio fabricated many of the furnishings himself from "very simple elements: iron tubes and plates, found wood and fabric." In fact, one of our favorite things at the Silvagnis' is a wardrobe that Giorgio cobbled together, using pieces from Irene's textile collection as the front panels. It's a perfect example of the creative collaboration between these two extraordinary people.

The thieves who made off with the Silvagnis' original furnishings also took a lot of paintings. "That's why we don't have a single painting hanging in our house, and why there are exposed frames with nothing inside—except for one painting in the dining room, a portrait of my great-grandmother," Giorgio explains. Actually, Giorgio would end up replacing the paintings lost in a very creative way: by painting the walls himself. He envisioned them coated with natural pigments, as is the custom in Italy, where he grew up. But upon hearing the painter's estimate, Giorgio decided the cost was too steep, and began doing the job himself. "When I was traveling to Rome on business, I always booked the Hotel de Ville a hundred yards away from the Villa Medici, to see how they restored the walls," he explains. "When I came back, I experimented by layering paint on a very

LEFT Giorgio's artistry is evident all over the dining room, from his hand-painted walls to his hand-crafted chandelier and the console he made out of an iron balcony railing.

small surface in one bathroom, and it came out very well. So then I became more sophisticated, using lighter pigments and adding more intense ones, and there it is!"

The effect is lovely, vaguely reminiscent of patinaed frescoes in ancient Rome, or Mark Rothko canvases. In one room, the walls are a deep terra-cotta to match one of Irene's treasured pottery urns. "She said, very poetically, 'I would like to have a room the color of the sunset'," Giorgio recalls. "So I mixed the pigments to match the urn."

The layout of objects is also important to Giorgio. "Sometimes," he admits, "I just need to move things." Does he ever: "I will buy vases, for example, and put them in the living room," Irene says, "and then I'll come in and find he's moved them around and rearranged them. I'll say, 'Well, you moved them,' and he'll say, 'Yes, they look better that way'!"

The tender loving care Irene and Giorgio have lavished on their house has brought them and their guests many years of delight, and deepened their attachment to each other. In France, a *maison de famille* is a house belonging to one family that is handed down from generation to generation.

With this house, the Silvagnis have put down a lifetime of roots in a relatively short time, to create the feeling of a true *maison de famille*.

LEFT A jar Irene found that matches her husband's hand-painted walls (top); Irene's ceramic collection with a piano bench that has gold-tipped legs that were crafted by Giorgio—a welcome surprise for Irene (bottom).
OPPOSITE The living room: an ideal spot for an afternoon nap.

FOLLOWING PAGES (64-65) Three views of the beautiful, restful master bedroom, a refuge for this couple who often entertain houseguests.

common grounds

harmonious how-to's

• Even when two lives mingle as stylishly as they do *chez* Irene and Giorgio, it is still important for both halves of a couple to feel they have a private space that is uniquely theirs. For Giorgio, it is the narrow swimming pool. When deciding the pool's measurements, he stretched out his arms and added an extra 15 centimeters on each side. "I am an egoist," he explains. "I like to swim alone!"

• The Do-It-Yourself movement is about more than just saving money. Creating wonderful furnishings or decorative flourishes with your own hands can make you look at your home with new eyes–and inspire exciting new projects.

• Recognizing a partner's quirks and accepting them with a smile can make home life interesting and fun. Irene is an irrepressible collector of things, but rather than try to restrain her, Giorgio greets each new acquisition with a joke. The teasing routine that ensues has become something of a kick for both of them.

OPPOSITE In the guest bedroom, his-and-hers photo portraits taken by different photographer friends at different times and places (Giorgio's picture was taken by François Halard and Irene's by Ferdinando Scianna) reveal a striking similarity.
LEFT Clockwise from top: Irene's growing collection of vintage textiles; in the dining room, resourceful Giorgio fashioned a lovely light fixture from a segment of railing from a Louis XIV stairway; the guest bathtub is canopied with sari fabric.

"We love doing houses together," says artist Nicholas Vega, who has been close to fashion designer Liza Bruce ever since the two first met as teenagers in high school. Now married, they continue their personal and professional love affair, and their extreme compatibility is evident in every interior they produce together. Besides designing Liza's stores over the years, Nicholas has also decorated the couple's homes in London, Jaipur, India, and St. Jean Cap Ferrat, the town on the French Riviera where they have a beautiful 1970s-era house.

The most amazing thing about this house is how quickly the couple managed to decorate it: The whole project took just nine weeks, from start to finish—"including the garden, which we ripped out and replanted, and the pool, which we re-tiled in Yves Klein blue," Nicholas says proudly. "You've got to be fearless; that's the key thing in life," he adds. That goes double for decorating under extreme time pressure.

For example: the lilac Roman shades that govern the light in the living room, and the matching lilac awning on the outside

partners in style

liza bruce & nicholas vega

of the window. "Nicholas had that idea, and I thought, that it was a very daring move," Liza admits. "But it proved to be exactly the correct motif for the whole mood of the villa." As it turned out, Nicholas knew exactly what he was doing: "Lilac works well there because it's a really calming color," he explains, "and it softens that intense Mediterranean light. So whatever time of day it is, you always get a soft light, like at dawn or dusk."

Although Liza tends to gravitate toward ethnic textiles and natural materials like wood, and Nicholas's taste leans more toward 1970s icons such as hot-pink, molded-plastic chairs by Werner Panton, their tastes create a stunning visual dynamic precisely *because* they are so different. "I'm very interested in symmetry and classicism, then he will contrast that," Liza explains. "We both understand that it's wonderful to contrast things, to let your imagination flow and to be surprised. Rather than having things be absolutely correct, we prefer to juxtapose pieces like the African sculptures sitting on the classic white 1970s table by Zanotta."

And so, a gilt-edged, marble-topped, rococo-style console table of Liza's looks perfectly at home beside the hard-edged metal chair that Nicholas fashioned of brass sheeting, and her decorative West African stool is the logical sidekick to the clean, spare lines of his white sofa. In the bedroom, the daring, scene-stealing walls that Nicholas painted by gradating color in large horizontal stripes are gentled by the splendid 19th-century bedspread from Uzbekistan. "The house can look very stark because of the strong colors," Liza says, "and traditional, primitive, pieces are included to soften the effect."

As Nicholas concludes, "We have very similar ideas about things. One of us might want to go crazier than the other, and it's a sort of balancing act. We hold each other in check where necessary—but not too much!"

A glamorous villa on the French Riviera

PRECEDING PAGES (68) In the living room, two enormous 1970s swivel chairs in orange and pink velvet found in London's Brick Lane, play up the vibrant colors of Nicholas's large-scale color-field paintings. He was inspired to apply this technique to the walls in several places around the house, including the master bedroom.

(70-71) Fuchsia chairs by Werner Panton surround the glass-topped dining table, called the Touring Table, designed by Gae Aulenti (left). In the living room, a happy blend of modern furnishings and primitive artifacts (right).
OPPOSITE Liza's marble-topped rococo table seems an unlikely match for Nicholas's bold, brass Chinoiserie chair and mirrored staircase uprisers—yet they work together.

LEFT The design of outdoor spaces was inspired by the couple's travels to Jaipur; Nicholas designed the concrete benches in the neo-Moghul style.
OPPOSITE A room with lots of reflection, which is courtesy of a mirrored ceiling and a white ceramic floor.

common grounds

harmonious how-to's

• "People are so fearful of what other people will think of the result, that they don't take a risk," Nicholas says. "But we have this motto: Risk everything, every day. And when in doubt, go for it, because your first instinct is usually right."

• Support your partner's vision. As long as your ideas are clearly structured, you can afford to be spontaneous too. "Don't hold each other back," Liza says. "Encourage each other to go for it!"

• Make use of mirrors wherever possible: they reflect light and make rooms look bigger, and enhancing the feeling of space always has a positive effect when two people live together. "I'm a big fan of mirrors," says Nicholas, who used them everywhere in the house, including the walls, wardrobes, and stairs.

LEFT Light bright: The abundant sun warms the high-tech kitchen with its contrasting Moroccan-style window screen (top) and the living room's metallic accents (bottom).
OPPOSITE Nicholas painted many of the walls in graded shades of soothing lilac—perfect for a bedroom.

Colombe Pringle is one of the world's great women of style. As the former editor-in-chief of French *Vogue*, she was responsible for such milestone magazines as the Christmas issues guest-edited by the Dalai Lama and Nelson Mandela. Today Colombe is editor-in-chief of *Maison Française*, and she and her husband, the equally elegant Jean Pierre Mahot de la Quérantonnais, share a fabulous 17th-century apartment on Paris's Left Bank.

This is the second marriage for both Colombe and Jean Pierre, which means each of them brought to this union the "stuff" of a mature, fully formed life: always a potential mine-field because of the emotional connections the pieces may have. What is remarkable about their place is how beautifully they've managed to combine items from both their pasts: big, masculine items and delicate feminine ones, antique artworks and contemporary ones by Richard Serra and Georg Baselitz. The effect is truly spectacular, with the kind of priceless, genuinely lived-in feel decorators strive to create.

Here's how they did it. "When we moved in together, I said to Mahot, Just don't be there when our stuff arrives," Colombe recalls. "So his stuff came, then mine came. And I got totally depressed, because nothing was fitting! So I sat in the drawing

uniting two lives

colombe pringle
& jean pierre mahot

A Paris apartment in the grand old style

PRECEDING PAGE (79)
A dramatic entrance: The foyer happily merges the couple's individual styles.
OPPOSITE Jean Pierre's office. The desk was made by Colombe's grandfather, André Groult. Behind it hangs a moumental print by Richard Serra.
RIGHT The "Madame Irma" sitting room (top); the focal point of Jean Pierre's office is a large-scale print by Anselm Kiefer that Colombe gave Jean Pierre for their tenth anniversary (bottom).

room and spoke to all these armchairs and things. I said, 'Now listen: You have to get on together. I'm *sure* we can make a story between all of you, so come on now, off we go.' And I started mixing everything." That fanciful approach practically guaranteed the result would be long on charm, and it is. "We call the drawing room the 'Madame Irma' room," Colombe says, "because it looks like a clairvoyant lives there!"

Of course, it doesn't take a crystal ball to divine that not every item of furniture would stand the test of time. "Some fell out because they didn't fit, but most of them did," says Colombe. That is no small achievement, considering that the couple's tastes come from two very different time periods. "Mahot is very 18th century," Colombe explains, "and he had much more money than me, so his things were very well done, with very expensive materials and all that—kilim armchairs, for example. I'm more 19th and 20th century: I love modern paintings, and I have lots of things from my grandfather, André Groult, a very well-known furniture designer of the 1920s."

Colombe and Jean Pierre did share one very important taste, however: a love of India. This helped unify the disparate elements of their conjugal decor. "I hate things that look formal," she says. "I hate that perfect 'total look.'" But where Colombe loves to improvise by throwing, say, an ethnic textile over a chair or slipcovering a sofa in brilliant purple silk, Jean Pierre had to overcome a tendency to overhaul his furnishings each time he moved. "I redid everything: curtains, upholstery . . . even the antiques were recovered to match the material on the walls. Colombe worked with what we had." Or, as she says, "He did it the grand way. I do it the artistic way!"

common grounds

harmonious how-to's

• When starting anew, resist the urge to put everything old away. Take Colombe's advice: "Try not to get rid of your old stuff just because you got rid of your old life. When you get married for the second time, you've learned a few things about life, so you don't have to like everything the other person likes— but you should accept the person's life before you—and that means his baggage." Who knows? Maybe you'll even grow to like your partner's taste.

• Don't give up on your eclectic furnishings if they don't imme- diately look like they're going to get along. "Move your things around for at least six months to make them fit," Jean Pierre says. "Give it six months before you give up, and don't be stingy with your time. Work it out!"

• If you expect to be mixing a lot of colorful objects, especially ones with radically different provenances, choose a unifying neutral scheme for the walls, like the white-trimmed Wedgwood gray in the "Madame Irma" sitting room.

• Yellow is an excellent color for the bedroom. "It's peaceful," Colombe explains, "and it's very flattering to the skin in both natural and electric light."

OPPOSITE Family portraits outside Colombe's pink powder room (top); an intimate collection of framed drawings, photographs, and some childhood souvenirs are displayed on Colombe and Jean Pierre's shared desk (bottom).

RIGHT Indian fabrics and a bowl of rose petals.

where the art is
april gornik &
eric fischl

In their 25-year relationship, artists Eric Fischl and April Gornik have displayed more than an impressive creative output. They have managed to do what few artist couples in history could achieve: They've found a way to live together while respecting each other's work, space, and need for creative independence. In this balanced marriage of talents, neither partner assumes dominance. Nowhere is this more evident than in the spectacular home they built in the Hamptons, which Eric designed together with his friend, the noted architect Lee Skolnick. With their Hamptons home, Eric and April have created a powerful, enduring symbol of their extraordinary partnership.

It is a truly inspiring space, a modernist fantasia of mahogany, concrete, steel, and glass that artfully combines Mediterranean, Japanese, and Arts and Crafts influences. Eric even built the first model for the house himself. But the most inspiring thing about this place, for us, is the gigantic twin studio spaces. Upon first approaching the property, one is struck by these two separate but adjoining structures, connected by a breezeway and sheathed in light-embracing glass. It is here that Eric and April work, separately yet together, connected yet respectful of each

other's need for privacy. In conceiving the place, Eric explains, "We had certain requirements: two studios, of course, of equal size. The footprints are identical, each 1,800 square feet, but the spaces are broken down differently, so my space feels smaller than April's even though it isn't. She needed a room separate from her paintings where she could do computer work. Also, because April is a gardener, we decided to create an outdoor space that was deer-proof and the office in her studio gives her a nice view of her gardens." The couple's requirements were as much symbolic as space-oriented. "The house had to express our relationship to each other and the rest of the world," Eric adds. "We put our work out there, and the fact that the studios are the first thing visitors see is a metaphor for that. The farther back into the complex you go, the more intimate and private it becomes. And in the farthest wing of the house is the master bedroom."

That bedroom, with its curvaceous platform bed (designed by Eric), has been immortalized in a series of Eric's recent paintings. Visitors to New York's Mary Boone Gallery were treated to several depictions of the couple's bedroom, which boasts an exquisite feature: an adjoining screened-in sleeping porch that is the height of romance in the summer. It takes a bit of walking to get to the bedroom, as April explains: "I think of the climb up to the bedroom as going up into a treehouse," she says. Adds Eric, "The house is spacious, but it feels intimate—which is a nice way of describing our relationship." The eclectic mix of furnishings throughout is another example of the couple's collaborative harmony. "We never used a decorator," April says. They don't need to: Their melange of fine furnishings old and new—including a silk-clad Indian daybed, a French 1940s chair, Franckesque sofas from Salon Moderne, mahogany cabinetry built by Eric's former assistant, Tom Brokish, a Thai

The home-studio the artists built in Sag Harbor, New York

PRECEDING PAGES
(89) The living room, with its majestic window.
(90) The entranceway with Eric's sculptures and a tranquil fountain set in the floor that he designed leads to April's splendid garden.
(91) The upstairs glassed-in library.
(92-93) The living room: a gallery of the couple's artist friends.
OPPOSITE The magnificent his-and-hers art studios inspire curiosity and admiration from visitors and passersby.
RIGHT Although equal in size, each atelier has been personalized: Eric's (top) feels smaller than April's (bottom) even though it is not.

bench, and a turn-of-the-century American sofabed, is as inspired as the design of the house itself. As for the art on the walls, "We mostly live with other people's work, because we live in our studios on a daily basis," Eric says.

"With the exception of April's large painting and my bronze sculpture of our late cat in the living room, mostly we have little things of ours in the house." The rest of their collection is comprised of the work of their artist friends, including Cindy Sherman, Malcolm Morley, Susan Rothenberg, David Salle, Ralph Gibson, Bryan Hunt, Sally Gall, and Erica Lennard.

Like anything worth waiting for, the path to the creation of a dream house such as this is never easy. Eric and April's project took more than two years of planning, conversation, and hard work. And yet, the only area where this couple disagreed involved a mundane matter indeed: the placement of the TV. "I wanted it in the kitchen," Eric says, "because we always eat dinner in front of the TV unless we have guests." April, on the other hand, thought that plan "gross" and got her way. "So now we take our food and go up to the TV room—all the way at the back of the house, under the bedroom!" Eric says with a laugh.

"Building a house is definitely a learning experience in a relationship," April observes. "It's a situation that demands a lot of discussion, decisions, aesthetics, financial pressure . . . For us this is a kind of extravagance we had never experienced before." Concludes her husband, obviously as taken with his mate as with the lavish home he built with her: "When I look at it, I don't see money; I see things that I love."

common grounds

harmonious how-to's

• The psychology of building a dream house is a complex one, as Eric and April learned. "There has to be a dominant and a recessive character," says Eric, but the latter should know that all the dominant half really wants, when they ask for guidance or an opinion, is a green light and a smile. "I kept trying to bring April into every decision I was making," Eric admits, "because I felt I needed her approval." Says April, "I was getting a mixed message. He didn't really want me to participate!" It's true, Eric concludes. "Advice to young homebuilders: Whoever is the force leading the thing, they're not asking for change. What they really want you to say is, OK! Fabulous! Go with it!"

• "Separate sinks are a luxury," Eric insists, "but separate bathrooms are frivolous." He should know: The master bath that he and April share has two cast-concrete basins because, she explains, "it's all about brushing your teeth when you want to."

• "Building a house is a defining experience," Eric says, "more so than renovating, because it's such a monumental project. It's an externalized, concretized version of what your interior dynamic is. It's two people trying to possess something equally, and it's something every couple should experience."

PRECEDING PAGES (96-97) The couple's bedroom appears in a series of Eric's recent paintings. The bed is designed by Eric and the rug is a collaboration between April and Denis Colomb. The shuttered door leads to the sleeping porch.
LEFT The main house, designed by Eric and his architect-friend Lee Skolnick, is a fantasia of mahogany, concrete, steel, and glass (top). The ultimate romantic bedroom: a screened-in sleeping porch (bottom).
OPPOSITE The fully-screened sitting room is perfect for taking in the country air—and, for Eric, enjoying a well-ventilated cigar.

If you have been lucky enough to receive a bouquet from New York's Zezé Flowers, you already know that artfully arranged flowers are the essence of romance. No matter how small or large, an arrangement put together by the one-name Brazilian floral designer is love in a vase. Now imagine what it might be like to live inside a Zezé arrangement every day of the year. It's a scenario Zezé and his wife Peggy don't have to imagine; they experience it every day at work together. They run Zezé's shop and share a glorious Manhattan townhouse with a magnificent garden. Here, no special occasion is required to justify the magic of flowers, and romance is in the air—indoors as well as out—seven days a week.

In this blooming bouquet of a home, the floral theme is pervasive. Of course there are fresh flowers, many of them thriving in pots or wooden boxes, including tulips, orchids, and amaryllis. But equally vibrant are the colorful, gold-framed flower prints and the black-and-white flower photographs, not to mention the flower-patterned lamps, vases, candelabra, and chandeliers. Flora also appears on the rugs and tapestries, on the embroidered and damask fabrics that cover many of the chairs, even on the stack of round boxes that hold Peggy's collection of vintage hats. A favorite recent acquisition is a 19th-century allegorical painting of Mother Earth holding violets in her hand. Pointing to a bookcase filled with illustrated tomes,

romance in *full bloom*

peggy & zezé

Peggy estimates that "probably ninety-nine percent of those books are about flowers."

There are many other nature-inspired details too, such as exquisite bronze birds, a gigantic wooden peacock that had a past life as a parade float, andirons in the shape of wise old owls, and lamps adorned with images of insects. In fact, this home displays a comprehensive appreciation of nature not seen since Art Nouveau took the decorative world by storm a century ago. But the focus is always on flowers, whether it's a silver candlestick shaped like entwined irises, or a just-bloomed ladyslipper orchid. "Flowers give you so much energy and add so much to your life," Zezé explains.

As befits people whose passion is to surround themselves with flowers, the couple loves to collect vases. They include an 18th-century porcelain ice bucket, Alvar Aalto's iconic wave vase, and a brilliant yellow and orange vessel made by a contemporary Brazilian glass artist. And not one of those vases stands empty. "Since we first met, I've sent her kilos and kilos of flowers," Zezé says. "It's a sure way to win someone over!" Peggy adds. "Now," Zezé says, "we're very fortunate to be surrounded by flowers all the time—at work and in our home."

Townhouse splendor in New York City's Chelsea

PRECEDING PAGE (101)
No corner of this home is left undecorated with flowers. Here, the couple's refreshing update on a traditional garden conservatory.

LEFT The dining room, with the original painted paneling and frescoes that inspired the couple to buy the house.
FOLLOWING PAGES
(104) The master bedroom's wine-dark Italian bedspread evokes the color of the couple's favorite orchid, *Pathiopedilum.*
(105) Peggy's love of vintage accessories is clearly in evidence in the dressing room from her collection of hat boxes and handbags to her crocodile suitcases.

common grounds

harmonious how-to's

• Whether a selection of flora arranged by a professional or a single stem, flowers bring instant romance into every home and blend with all types of decor. Who doesn't love flowers–and what better way to celebrate the love that brought you together?

• If you and your partner don't agree to go all the way with chintz or lushly patterned furnishings, there are many other ways to bring the romantic, relaxing benefits of flowers into your home. Topiaries are easier to maintain than cut blooms; fine pot-pourri has a wonderful, long-lasting aroma; and delicately scented candles provide an instant atmospheric lift. One caveat: with scented products, choose a fragrance that you both can agree on. Rose, for instance, can be a little too feminine; instead try something exotic, such as amber.

• A florist's eye for detail can glamorize even the most mundane aspects of your home. At Zezé and Peggy's home, the logs in the fireplaces are beautiful white birch.

LEFT AND OPPOSITE
Everywhere in their home from the hearth to the living room, this couple surrounds themselves with *objets* that they equally adore.

bohemian brilliance

michele lamy & rick owens

Michele Lamy and Rick Owens are cut from the same hipster cloth. She is a devastatingly chic former fashion designer who now runs the L.A. restaurant Les Deux Cafés, which is a favorite of many Hollywood celebrities. He is a much talked-about young fashion designer known for his edgy, offbeat designs, which, he says, "are an extension of the way I look at Michele. She has this really amazing balance of elegance and primitive instinct that's always fascinated me, so my clothes are sophisticated and crude mixed together." Little wonder Michele proudly exclaims, "I only wear Rick's clothes." They were created with her in mind, and they look wonderful on her.

Together, Michele and Rick have designed a home that is as unique as they are, joining three old storefronts located directly across the street from Les Deux Cafés (one of them, formerly known as The Baroque Bookstore, belonged to a friend of Charles Bukowski nicknamed "Red" for his Communist leanings). It is a unique live/work arrangement, for it is also Rick's studio, as you can tell by the many gowns on display, hanging from industrial racks and draped on dress forms. But it is also something of a performance-art set, complete with the original

peeling walls and concrete floors that came with each property, which the couple deliberately left unchanged.

Because of their proximity to Michele's restaurant, the couple didn't bother installing a kitchen or formal dining area. "If we have a party, we have it in the restaurant," Michele says. Adds Rick, "Les Deux Cafés is kind of our dining room. We don't eat at home—there's no point, because she has the most incredible restaurant across the street." In fact, the "dining area" actually serves as a "dyeing area" where Rick experiments with the artisanal hand-dyed fabrics for which he's known, and the drinking glasses are actually recycled dyptique candle jars. Not everyone could deal with such a singular lifestyle, but Michele and Rick know exactly what they like and what they need. "We just don't want to deal with dishes," he says. "We don't even have a microwave. My parents visit and say, 'Where do you keep the paper towels?' And I can't imagine having anything as prosaic as paper towels lying around!"

There's still more originality on display in the bedroom, a room Rick covered in sound-absorbent charcoal-colored felt, in homage both to the conceptual artist Joseph Beuys and the author Marcel Proust. ("Talk about pretentious!" he says with a laugh.) Halogen lights are built into the headboard for nighttime reading, and treasured books and magazines are stuffed haphazardly onto the shelves of a tall, bulging bookcase, which also holds a TV. The room has an amazing sense of privacy and isolation, "like a bunker," Michele explains. "That's important to us, because every other space we have is completely open to the public." According to Rick, "The whole place is a very per-

sonal mingling, an extension of the way I look at Michele. Everything we do is a combination of us. Michele is very instinctual and volatile; I'm very placid and methodical. I like to reduce things down to the basics, and Michele's very poetic and dramatic. I think it was one of the cleverest things I ever did in my life, to connect with someone who complements how practical I can be! The way the studio looks is a mix of her drama and my wanting to keep things minimal."

"I thought it would be sort of temporary at first," Michele admits, "while I was building the restaurant and Rick was building his business. But now we're never going to move: This is home. It's a natural way for us to live," she says. "Before this, we used to live in hotels a lot; for a couple of years, we lived at the Chateau Marmont [the L.A. inn renowned for its glamorously grungy appeal]. We don't like to divide our lives between work and home; we like to keep things flowing."

"I think we're really lucky," Rick concludes. "We have a really idyllic lifestyle—kind of like living in a barn or a cave. Actually, I call it the cave, because that's the way it is: primitive and gray. I manufacture in Italy, and I show the clothes in Paris or New York, so I'm back and forth between here and Europe a lot, where I stay in fancy hotels with Murano chandeliers and floral damasks. Michele and I talk on the phone every night, and she'll say, 'You're probably not going to want to come back home to our cave, because you're living in brocade and damask!' And I'm like, 'Are you kidding?' That's exacty *why* I want to come back: I love the contrast, but I definitely prefer the severity of home."

In Los Angeles,
three storefronts
equal one unique
living arrangement

PRECEDING PAGES (108)
One of Rick's recent fashion
designs is displayed on a dress
form. A view to his atelier is in
the background.
(110) The living area opens onto
an overgrown alleyway—a stark
contrast to the cashmere-covered
chairs and sofa.
(112-113) Michele's dressing
room, with Rick's larger-then-life
portrait of her and a friend,
where she puts on her choice of
his designs which hang from
industrial-strength garment racks
(left and right).
LEFT The bedroom, cloaked in
dark gray cashmere.

common grounds

harmonious how-to's

• If you are artistically inclined, it can be incredibly romantic to include a monument to your love in your home. In Michele's closet hangs a large painting Rick made, based on an old photograph of Michele. "It was one of those really great pictures," he says, "so I re-did it huge for her birthday."

• If you know you don't intend to perform certain activities at home, such as cooking, don't install major appliances you know you'll never use just because convention dictates one "should" live with them.

• An avant-garde lifestyle often involves certain practical pitfalls, so always be easygoing and remember to accentuate the positive. "People are always surprised that we did without hot water for two years," Rick points out. "We used to hose each other off in the back alley, and in winter we'd shower at the gym."

LEFT A stuffed monkey was Michele's birthday gift to Rick (top). Michele's restaurant, Les Deux Cafés, across the street from the couple's living quarters, is where they dine (bottom). **OPPOSITE** The dining-dyeing table, where Rick experiments with fabric colors. On it are lit candles and empty candle holders, the latter also serve as drinking glasses.

Together, they run a Los Angeles event and interior design firm called Aqua Vitae, and it would be hard to find a young couple more spirited than Alexandra and Eliot Angle. As Alexandra puts it, "We have a similar style—we're both sentimental about family things, but we're also interested in new design. Plus, we both appreciate a sense of humor in things." All three facets of their shared personal style are evident throughout their 1940s house, which they recently designed and renovated, and where they now live and do business.

"We both fell in love with this house the second we saw it," Alexandra says. "The house itself had very good bones, and we loved the location. We have three-hundred-and-sixty-degree views of the Hollywood Hills, the San Gabriel mountains, and downtown L.A.!"

Before they met, they led very different lives. "I traveled all the time," Alexandra says. "I'm obsessed with moving, and the fact that I was constantly on the move obviously affected my

L.A. effervescence

alexandra & eliot angle

style of furniture. In Japan, I had Japanese furniture. In the old townhouse where I lived in Portland, Maine, I had antique Victorian things." Then she met Eliot, who happens to have a lot of family heirlooms: tables, chairs, lots of old books, and silver. This helped awaken Alexandra's heirloom instinct, giving her a new appreciation for the furnishings handed down through her family, like the antique cabinet from her grandmother's basement that now lives in the couple's dining room, and the imposing portrait of Alexandra's great-great-great Aunt Lydie, which presides over the living room from its spot above the fireplace.

Fittingly for a couple that produces memorable cocktail parties for a living, the Angles' place boasts an enviable bar, fully stocked with attractive glassware handed down from both their families, as well as the collection of vintage shakers, strainers, and decanters they've gathered together.

"When we first started living together," Alexandra explains, "we started to restore a lot of old family stuff that we both had inherited. That was our focus: how to use these pieces in a contemporary setting. We had a lot of beautiful things—they just needed a lot of attention." Like the 18th-century French mahogany table the couple found in the chicken barn at Alexandra's uncle's house. "It was in very bad shape," she says. Now, in its glorious restored state, it occupies a place of honor in the study (which doubles as a sunroom).

"Both of our families are from New England," Eliot says, "so there are all these attics we can pilfer, especially with older relatives who just don't want all these things. It's been a real privilege, like having our own little flea market, but much more meaningful! That's been quite influential to our style, I think. And it brings a whole romance to design, when you use things that have been passed down through different family members."

Besides sending treasured heirlooms to the furniture restorer, Alexandra and Eliot also regularly collaborate—she designs, he gamely builds—on do-it-yourself projects that are sure to be heirlooms for future generations. His talent for building things is something Eliot admits he wouldn't have discovered without his wife's encouragement. "I wouldn't say I'm a master carpenter," he says, modestly. "But I started wanting to make things because of our mutual interest in design, which she helped me to develop."

Among Eliot's creations are the impressive, angular, "Japanese-contemporary-style" decks in the garden and the queen-size platform bed in the master bedroom. "It's a pretty crude design," he says of the bed, "but we wanted a very stark, almost Asian feel, so I made it out of fourteen-inch wood beams and painted it charcoal gray. It took a fair amount of trial and error, off and on for about a week," he adds. "And there were definitely some trips to Home Depot and then more trips, when it wasn't working out. But it was really fun to make."

Across from the bed is an unusual bedroom feature: a Kohler bathtub big enough for two. "That was my idea," Alexandra explains. "I love taking baths. And I've always wanted a bathtub in the bedroom because it seemed incredibly romantic to me." It has proved quite romantic: Although he's a shower person, Eliot went along with the bath-in-the-bedroom idea and the couple now bathe together about twice a week.

A renovated house in Los Angeles

PRECEDING PAGE (119)
The living room, dominated by an imposing portrait of Alexandra's great-great-great Aunt Lydie.

ABOVE A beautiful table setting
created by a couple who make
entertaining an art and a business.

common grounds

harmonious how-to's

• If one half of a couple agrees to a design feature to please the other half, it's nice to return the favor. Eliot made a concession to Alexandra's love of baths, and she acknowledged his love of showers in the master bathroom—a massive, open shower tiled in dark gray slate, a nod to the dominant color of the landscape in New York City, Eliot's beloved hometown. This is one couple that really knows how to bathe in style: The shower also features a full-length window that affords a fine vantage point on the house's spectacular view. "It's kind of great to stand in the shower and look out at the hills," Eliot says. "It's a little racy, but the property is situated so that no houses can really look in!"

• Two sinks in a shared bathroom can be a simple formula for harmony that more and more couples are incorporating into their living arrangements. "It's nice to have individual sink space," Alexandra explains. "That way, you're not crowding each other out."

• If you don't have sufficient basement or barn space, consider renting a storage unit. Besides keeping your living space free of clutter (which is a common source of conflict between couples) it enables you to hold on to things you might give away in haste and regret later. The Angles currently store several pieces of furniture and miscellaneous items, many from their respective families, which they felt simply didn't work in their current surroundings. "I'm sure they will appear in other places," Alexandra says.

PRECEDING PAGES (122-123) Two glimpses of the house's extraordinary views. The farmhouse dining room table was recycled from their previous house in Maine.

LEFT The bar with a collection of vintage decanters and glasses (top). Bathing beauty: Individual sinks provide convenience (bottom).
OPPOSITE A tub in the bedroom (Alexandra's idea) is pure indulgence.

when a house chooses you

annie kelly & tim street-porter

Tim Street-Porter and Annie Kelly intrigued us even before we met them, because we have something very basic in common: Like us, they are a photographer–interior designer duo. They are such frequent flyers, it's safe to say these two are even more nomadic than we are! Besides shooting some of the world's most beautiful homes for shelter magazines and books, Tim also happens to be a trained architect. Not surprisingly, the homes he and his wife have created together are always visually stunning: extremely photogenic tableauxs of beautifully-arranged objects, auction-house finds, travel souvenirs, and family mementos.

A perfect example is the place they currently call home, Villa Vallombrosa, a Mediterranean-style historic landmark in Los Angeles that was previously home to many well-known people, including the actress Janet Gaynor, the photographer Baron De Meyer, and the composer Leonard Bernstein. Tim and Annie were in the market for a 1950s-era home, but they fell hard as soon as they saw this architectural treasure from the 1920s. "Tim and I did not even discuss whether we should buy this house—it was so obvious," Annie recalls. "We just knew as soon as we walked in. It was a simultaneous revelation, as it were!"

In fact, the house has succeeded in keeping this extremely peripatetic duo grounded (well, almost). "It's probably what kept us in L.A.," Tim notes. "We've always been tempted to go and live in Paris, or New York, or Mexico." Adds Annie, "It's such an unusual and attractive house to live in. If we had a more ordinary house, I don't know if we'd have stayed in L.A. as long as we have."

You would think two people as aesthetically oriented—and opinionated—as Tim and Annie would move in and immediately set about changing everything to their taste. Well, they didn't. Many of the features they saw when they first looked at the house are still there, "as is," including the red paint on the walls of the sitting room and the silvery damask wallpaper in the master bedroom. This was a conscious decision, in order to preserve the original spirit of the house. Restraint can pay off. "A lot of stuff we didn't change, because the people who'd done the main renovation had captured the spirit of the house quite well," Annie remarks. "We did make a few modifications," she allows, "like adding some painted friezes here and there, and taking away a few, and repainting a guest bedroom. Not bad after twelve years!"

These two agree on the most important aspect of furnishing an architecturally important home. As Tim puts it, "a house should be furnished in relationship to its style—the interior has to relate to the exterior."

Now, thanks to their loving attention to detail, the house's interior is both true to its architectural style and a uniquely personal reflection of Tim and Annie's exquisite tastes. Interestingly, although the place was built in the 1920s, the couple has decorated mostly with 18th-century furnishings, because they felt the architect's aim was to create the feeling of a classic Italian villa. "Eighteenth-century furniture is what

really works in this house," Annie explains. "Anything older than that is too heavy, and anything newer doesn't seem true to the original architectural intention of the house."

With two pairs of creative eyes at work, whose vision wins out? "I'm more likely to find things for the house," Annie explains, "because as a decorator I'm out and about, and going to auctions. I've been lucky: I've rarely found anything that Tim hasn't really liked. When I bring something back, then we decide together where it should go. But sometimes, I think you have to realize that if you're a couple and one person is a decorator or an architect, or at all involved in design, the other person really has to cut them a bit more slack and let them take the lead. As an interior designer, it's so important to be able to practice on your own house; after all, you can't practice on your clients!"

Keeping the flame in a Hollywood Hills landmark

PRECEDING PAGES (126) Loving flourishes: 18th-century Portuguese candlesticks flank an assortment of objects and fresh flowers, backed by a 19th-century embroidered panel that hangs from the 20-foot ceilings of the Villa Vallombrosa, Annie and Tim's 1920s home.
(128-129) Two views of the Venetian courtyard with its romantic Romeo-and-Juliet balcony, designed by Nathan Coleman.

(130-131) The living room, furnished with 18th- and 19th-century French furniture; the tall front window is draped in a pair of Indian wedding saris.
OPPOSITE Against the vibrant orange walls that came with the house, a 16th-century portrait hangs above a Napoleon III sofa.
RIGHT Intimate spaces: a corner of the sitting room (top) seen from the central courtyard and a dining area in front of the sunny sitting room (bottom), used mainly in winter.

common grounds

harmonious how-to's

• When buying an architectural treasure, don't assume you have to overhaul everything just to put your stamp on it. Chances are, the previous residents had a few worthwhile ideas you can inherit! You might even luck out.

• Avoid being *too* literal when trying to re-create a specific look for a specific style of house. Annie recalls buying 1920s-era reproduction Empire chairs and bringing them home, only to realize "they just weren't right—even though the chairs were the same age as the house." Remember, it's about getting the right flavor, not necessarily amassing things from one specific time period.

• "I think each person has to feel a sense of belonging to the house," Annie wisely points out. Make sure you each have your own territory to retreat to: "something that's particularly yours, even if it's just a comfy chair by the fire you can return to at the end of the day."

• Consider minimizing time spent watching television. "I think TV detracts from your private time to eat and talk and read," says Tim.

LEFT In the bedroom, the couple's treasured photographs of family and pets (top). The library boasts a large collection of research books, which Tim consulted to write his own books, including *Casa Mexicana* (bottom).

OPPOSITE Popsie, the cat, rarely leaves the master bedroom, which has not changed at all and still sports its original damask wallpaper.

It's a challenge faced by many urban couples: How do you make an architecturally unremarkable apartment feel like home? Jenna Lyons and Vincent Mazeau knew they wanted to impart a feeling of warmth to their boringly boxy L-shaped Manhattan loft, and they've managed to create an interior that is as welcoming as it is well designed.

Design is very important to both halves of this creative couple. She works as a fashion designer; he is an artist and partner at Big Room, a design collective that creates sets for TV commercials, music videos, and fashion photography (including a shoot with Brad Pitt for *W* magazine). Their first date was spent discussing and designing a table on wheels that they later built together, and their place is accented with intriguing details such as an oddly beautiful "wineglass doorbell" by Droog Design, a 300-psi electromagnet that locks the bathroom door, and a sleek sand-colored Zanotta sofa purchased at Moss, the Manhattan resource for ultra-modern furnishings.

Not surprisingly, when it came to laying down the concrete that's quite popular in loft circles, they were uncompromising in

loft living with love

jenna lyons &
vincent mazeau

their vision of the perfect flooring, and sent their contractor to a concrete-floored art gallery to see an example. The unusual sandblasted glass wall in the bathroom, meanwhile, was an idea Vincent hit on after seeing something similar at the Helmut Lang boutique in Manhattan.

With so many trendy elements, their place could have ended up cooler-than-thou, but instead it feels genuinely cozy. That warmth is generated by certain key details: a 100-year-old wooden dining table from France . . . a hammock they brought home from a vacation in Mexico . . . a Bakshaish rug from Afghanistan . . . and a gigantic chandelier crafted of elk antlers. It gives off a soft glow that's infinitely more romantic than the hard, flat light found in most halogen-flooded loft spaces. "It was my obsession—there's something so not New York about it," Jenna explains of the very rustic-looking fixture that's the last thing one would expect to find in a space like this. Vincent admits he was surprised when the antler issue first reared its head. "When I first saw it I was like, are you serious?" he recalls. "Even being more of the cowboy, I didn't understand the gesture. It took me a little while, but now I love it."

He warmed up to the chandelier enough to spend hours devising a way to disassemble the thing and put it back together after it turned out, upon delivery, that it wouldn't fit through the door. "It was like trying to get an octopus in the front door," Vincent says. "We had to store it," Jenna remembers. "I was so upset. Then one night at dinner, Vincent surprised me. He said, 'It's in.' That was so sweet, I burst into tears!"

In the brick-walled bedroom alcove, the unlikely focal point is a feature that's at once industrial-chic and fuzzy: steel clothing racks that hold the couple's clothes ("of which ninety-nine percent are Jenna's," Vincent reports with an accepting shrug). He clearly appreciates his wife's sartorial aesthetic, describing the closet as "a combination of functional closet and museum for archiving fashion." To help make her daily selection easier, he put an LCD screen, "smaller than a shoebox," on the floor and catalogued image files on it of Jenna's impressive shoe collection.

Another high-tech token of esteem is on display in the kitchen. The couple calls it the "Tower of Power," and it was designed by Vincent to hold alcohol, spices, gourmet oils, vinegars, and other edibles. The Tower even features his-and-hers coffee makers, with a special slide-out tray to accommodate Jenna's machine of choice, a Krups drip that wakes her with freshly-brewed java (Vincent, whose work schedule permits him to rise later than his wife, drinks espresso made with a Gaggia, and brings her espresso in bed on weekend mornings; he cooks, too).

"He was at Zabar's, on his hands and knees, measuring coffee makers," she recalls of the effort spent on designing the Tower. "That's definitely love." Observing the mutual admiration in this couple's eyes, even a cynical observer would have trouble disagreeing with that. "There's something so special when someone embraces the differences between you," Jenna says. Vincent agrees: "Anybody designing a relationship would be wrong to say that it's based only on similarities. Of all the ways that Jenna and I are attracted to each other, a good part are the ways that we're different."

A loft in downtown New York City

RIGHT The couple's personal tribute to 9/11 on the huge bulletin board above their communal home-office.

common grounds

harmonious how-to's

• Lavish attention on your bathroom; in an urban cookie-cutter space, it's an extremely personal retreat. "We congregate in our bathroom in the morning," Jenna explains. "He's shaving, I'm showering, and it's so comfortable. It's become a really intimate morning ritual for us."

• Go together to public spaces for inspiration on finishes: They're an excellent design resource. "Whether it be the Marc Jacobs store, the Dia Center for Arts, or the Hudson Hotel, a public space can inspire you and serve as a perfect reference point for the contractor you're working with," Vincent says. "Tearsheets from magazines are one thing to interpret, but real surfaces—particularly large expanses—most clearly represent all the subtleties you're after."

• Do whatever you can to make the lighting feel soft. "Purely on a physiological level, it's really important to have a sense of access to natural light or the sky or a view," Vincent says, "especially in New York."

• Happy accidents are OK. "Going with the flow can be painful, but it can have pleasant surprises," Vincent says. Adds Jenna, "It's ironic that all we ever tried to do was hide this huge rack of clothes, and now it's become a focal point!"

PRECEDING PAGES (136) Jenna's beloved antler chandelier hangs over the dining area of this contemporary urban space. The kitchen has concrete slab counters and a huge blackboard. **(138-139)** The living area sports a quirky detail: a hammock that the couple loves crowding into.

OPPOSITE Metal scaffolding for the huge exposed his-and-hers closet.
LEFT His-and-hers coffee makers set in the "Tower of Power," a shelving unit that Vincent designed to hold kitchen accessories (top). The bathroom, a favorite communal space (bottom).

designing the ultimate love nest

jackie yellin & julie milligan

It could be the premise for an update of *Green Acres*. A divorce lawyer turned award-winning landscape designer, Julie Milligan adores city living, while her partner, real-estate developer Jackie Yellin, hates the city and prefers the country. Or, as Julie puts it, "I'm urban, but a remote town of thirty-five would be fine with Jackie." With their two residences, a condo with terrace and roof garden in Santa Monica, California, and a house on the Hawaiian island of Kauai, this resourceful couple has achieved the most stylish compromise imaginable, sharing and enjoying the best of two very different worlds.

Division of labor is one secret to their success. "You need to pick the spaces that are really important to you," Jackie explains. "If the kitchen or bathroom is more important to one partner, then that should be their final decision. But you do need to communicate with each other and respect the other person's opinion, because you don't want to have something in the house that somebody absolutely hates. That's not fun!"

They consult each other on major decisions, of course. But the outdoor spaces are Julie's domain—which makes sense because she's the gardener—while Jackie, who has decorated many homes for friends and clients, takes the lead in designing

the interiors. For this couple, clearly splitting responsibilities has proven to be a recipe for harmony. "When we're in Kauai, we cook fabulous romantic dinners," Julie explains. "Although we both love to cook, Jackie has evolved to be more of the cook. We always say that she's food and I'm mood! I do the hors d'oeuvres, light the candles and torches, get out all the linens, and set the table." Adds Jackie, "It's like living with Martha Stewart—if Julie sets a table, it's gorgeous."

The most important ingredient of Julie and Jackie's enviable harmony is good old-fashioned true love. In their Kauai home, tributes to their feelings for each other crop up everywhere, from the blackboard in the upstairs office, where they leave each other notes, to the iron J's (their shared first initial) set into the garden path.

Their urbane Santa Monica condo brings the outdoors in with an eclectic, Asian-modern vibe. Many charming features include maple floors, seagrass carpets, a bookcase that's an old canoe, and a screen made out of twigs. The interiors are the remarkably seamless result of opposite approaches to shopping. "When we first did the condo, I could've furnished it in two days," Jackie recalls. "Julie kept telling me to slow down. We went back and looked at our bed five times before buying it."

The couple's "high-tech barn" on Kauai is a fantasia of industrial-strength metal, concrete, wood, glass, and cement in a lush tropical setting. It is truly a romantic paradise. "Jackie and I designed the house ourselves," Julie says. "It's clearly built for a couple: There are no guest bedrooms, it's all one big, open room, and that was intentional. When we first started living together, in Aspen, Jackie's house had five bedrooms and five baths, and we have a lot of friends and family, so people were always staying with us. We love our friends and relatives, but after a few years we realized we'd never had dinner alone

A custom-built home on the Hawaiian island of Kauai

PRECEDING PAGES (144)
The couple's herb garden in Kauai, created by Julie, a passionate gardener. Two iron J's, the couples' shared first initials, are set in the concrete path.
(146-147) The once-controversial chartreuse sofa is the living room's dazzling focal point in the couple's "high-tech barn" in Kauai, which is surrounded by verdant gardens.
(148) On Kauai, two giant chairs give a lifeguard's vantage point for viewing sunsets over the Pacific Ocean.
(149) Kauai's palm-shaded herb garden, designed by Julie, with a

Balinese hut in the center. For Jackie's birthday, Julie created a cozy bed for a special overnight outing in the garden.
(150) A bronze screen brings privacy to the sleeping space in Kauai.
(151) The upstairs in the couple's Kauai home is part workspace, part bedroom.
ABOVE AND OPPOSITE
The bathroom, with double sinks and over-size wall and ceiling showers in Kauai. The couple designed a unique tub, with an overflow feature, comfortable enough for two.

together in our own home! So we built the house in Kauai as a place for two people: a sexy, intimate space for a couple to share. And we love it."

Out of what used to be an eight-acre plot of overgrown weeds, Julie has created a verdant oasis of ornamental grasses and trees. The jazzy chartreuse sofa in the living room is a beautiful foil for the dazzling greenery on the terrace beyond. But that sofa was a point of controversy at first. Jackie, who makes decorating decisions with great speed and confidence, met resistance not just from the more deliberate Julie, but from the salesperson as well.

"Julie said, 'You can't get that,' and the lady in the store said 'Are you crazy?' But I get these visions, and I envisioned it as being perfect." To be safe, Jackie ordered two sets of slip-covers, one in a more conservative stone green. "I told Julie that if she didn't like the other color it's not the end of the world—it's just fabric. Besides, it's fun to change things. And now she absolutely loves the bright green."

Their Kauai home permits all activities—dining, showering, even sleeping—to happen outside, where the temperature hovers between 70 and 80 degrees at all times. Julie still spends some of her time in her beloved Southern California, while Jackie spends most of hers in nature, far from the city. What a happy arrangement for a city mouse and her country counterpart!

"Jackie and I love spending time together, and I think that's essential. I used to be the most independent, self-sufficient person on Earth, and now I'm not quite the same without her. We have an incredible respect for each other's design talents, which is why we were able to do all this, on an island, away from everybody."

154

common grounds

harmonious how-to's

• "Building a home together creates stress," Jackie says. During the process, remember to be kind to each other, and spend as much time as your hectic schedule allows on relaxing activities. "The key to surviving construction," Julie offers, "is a good sense of humor and a lot of good wine! The happiest moment of every day for us was sitting down with a bottle from Jackie's collection."

• If one of you is bold about color and pattern but the other is not, don't take risks on things like tile and flooring that are difficult to replace. Apply daring ideas to items that can be easily changed without great expense or heartbreak, such as slipcovers and curtains.

• "When you design a home from scratch, it costs more money than you ever think," says Jackie. "Even rich people are broke when they're done! So I always advise people to buy furniture while they're building. Besides, your house will never look as charming or as warm if you just go out and buy everything at the end. Collecting along the way makes everything feel like a process."

PRECEDING PAGES (154) Kauai's formal dining arrangement, with Jackie's wine collection. **(155)** With so many places in which to eat, the couple can select a setting to match the cuisine and season. **LEFT** In their Santa Monica residence, stones and shells with special meaning for the couple are displayed in a box (top); the wooden suitcases-on-wheels were Jackie's first purchase upon moving in with Julie (bottom). **OPPOSITE** A lush private terrace with stone floors and a tropical outdoor shower just outside the bathroom in Kauai, created by Julie.

10 STEPS

=

HARMONIOUS

+

LIVING

Ten Steps to Harmonious Living

1. Create individual spaces of your own: Make sure you each have your own personal space.

2. Consider moving as a means to a fresh start.

3. Mutual respect is essential.

4. Be wary of trends, yet don't be afraid to experiment.

5. Listen to the voice of a professional.

6. Divide up responsibilities to achieve your goals.

7. Don't feel pressured to design and furnish every aspect of the place before you move in.

8. Remember your tastes will change and evolve along with your relationship.

9. Follow your dreams.

10. And don't forget to have fun!

Photography copyright © 2002 Erica Lennard
Artistic Director: Denis Colomb
Text copyright © 2002 Julia Szabo

PROJECT EDITOR: SANDRA GILBERT WITH ELAINE SCHIEBEL
PRODUCTION MANAGER: PAMELA SCHECHTER
DESIGNER: IVETTE MONTES DE OCA

Published by Stewart, Tabori & Chang
A Company of La Martinière Groupe
115 West 18th Street
New York, NY 10011

Export Sales to all countries except Canada, France, and French-speaking
Switzerland:
Thames and Hudson Ltd.
181A High Holborn
London WCIV 7QX
England

Canadian Distribution:
Canadian Manda Group
One Atlantic Avenue, Suite 105
Toronto, Ontario M6K 3E7
Canada

Library of Congress Cataloging-in-Publication Data

Lennard, Erica.
    Living together : how couples create harmony at home / by Erica Lennard
and Denis Colomb with Julia Szabo.
        p. cm.
    ISBN 1-58479-223-X
    1. Interior decoration—History—20th century. 2. Artist
couples—Dwellings—History—20th century. I. Colomb, Denis. II. Szabo, Julia,
1965- III. Title.
    NK2115.3.A78 L46 2002
    747.2'049—dc21
2002021170

The text of this book was composed in Centaur and Interstate.
Printed in Italy

1 3 5 7 9 10 8 6 4 2
First Printing

Acknowledgments

To Marie Jeanne and Joseph Colomb

Thanks to all the couples who opened their homes and
their hearts to us and to some of our special friends
who helped us along the way: Laurie Frank, Valerie
Pasquiou, Brooks Adams and Lisa Liebman, Konstantin
Kakanias, and Susan Penzner. Thanks to our assistants
for their help on the photo shoots: Tobias in New York,
Gaetan in Paris, and Patty in Los Angeles.

Thanks also to Suzy Slesin, who inadvertently brought
us together; to our agent, Helen Pratt, for her support;
to our editor, Sandy Gilbert, for her tireless efforts; to
Ivette Montes de Oca for her beautiful design; and to
Julia Szabo for helping us capture in words all of our
ideas about harmonious living.

In the midst of this project and on our way to a photo
shoot, we were in New York City on September 11, 2001,
and we would like to dedicate this book to all New
Yorkers, for their courage then and now.

Picture Captions

Front cover: The lavender bedroom at Liza Bruce and Nicholas Vega's bedroom
on the French Riviera. Back cover: (from left to right) In Alexandra and Eliot
Angle's Los Angeles home, the bathtub is located in an unusually romantic place:
the couple's bedroom; the hammock lends a quirky coziness to Jenna Lyons and
Vincent Mazeau's Manhattan loft; Liza Bruce and Nicholas Vega enjoy their
dazzling custom-tiled blue swimming pool; a collection of 1960s vases are the
only decorative objects in Florence Baudoux and Aldo Fabiani's minimalist Paris
apartment. Title page: (top) At the Provençal home of Irene and Giorgio Silvagni,
his-and-hers portraits taken by different photographer friends; (bottom) Annie
Kelly and Tim Street-Porter's charming Romeo-and-Juliet balcony in the courtyard of their Los Angeles home. Page 2: (clockwise from top left) Giorgio
Silvagni's hand-painted this wall, which makes a dramatic backdrop for the daybed
covered in textiles collected by his wife Irene; the focal point of Jenna Lyons and
Vincent Mazeau's dining room is an enormous antler chandelier that Jenna loved
at first sight; April Gornik and Eric Fischl's handsome master bedroom served as
inspiration for a recent series of paintings by Eric; The capacious mirrored closet
that Ashley Hicks built for his wife Allegra in their London townhouse. Page 3:
A bookshelf and metal benches in Irene and Giorgio Silvagni's guest bedroom are
the result of Giorgio's creative handiwork.

HARMONY